EVENTS THAT CHANGED YOUR WORLD

THE WRIGHT BROTHERS TAKE THEIR FIRST FLIGHT

by Rachel Werner

PEBBLE
a capstone imprint

Published by Pebble, an imprint of Capstone
1710 Roe Crest Drive, North Mankato, Minnesota 56003
capstonepub.com

Library of Congress Cataloging-in-Publication Data is available on the Library of Congress website.

ISBN: 9780756581169 (hardcover)
ISBN: 9780756581527 (paperback)
ISBN: 9780756581220 (ebook PDF)

Summary: It's easy to get to many places around the world these days—we can just fly there. But in the early 1900s, it wasn't so simple. But the Wright brothers were up to the challenge of figuring out how people could fly. Learn about the impact of the first flight on the history of aviation.

Editorial Credits
Editor: Ericka Smith; Designer: Terri Poburka; Media Researcher: Svetlana Zhurkin; Production Specialist: Katy LaVigne

Image Credits
Alamy: North Wind Picture Archives, 7, Science History Images, 10; Getty Images: Archive Photos/FPG/Paul Thompson, 22, Archive Photos/Graphic House, 21, Archive Photos/Pictorial Parade, 26, Fox Photos, 23, Heritage Images/National Motor Museum, 11, MPI, 25, Westend61, cover (top); Library of Congress: cover (bottom), 5, 8, 9, 13, 15, 17, 18, 20, 28; NASA: Joel Kowsky, 27; Shutterstock: Everett Collection, 19

Printed and bound in the USA. PO 5853

TABLE OF CONTENTS

Words in **bold** are in the glossary.

Dreams of Flying

In the early 1900s, the Wright brothers dreamed of flying. After years of experimenting, they built the first airplane that could fly.

Their dreams changed how people could explore the world. Since then, the airplane has shortened trips across land and sea.

The Wright brothers' invention changed travel. And they paved the way for others to reimagine where we could go.

Orville Wright

Wilbur Wright

Getting There and Back

Different types of transportation have helped people get themselves—and things like clothes, food, and medicine—from one place to another across land. For centuries, people needed animals like horses, donkeys, and camels to travel long distances.

In the 1800s, people invented many new **vehicles**. The first bicycles, trains, cars, and trolleys were all created during this time.

After people started using steam to power boats in the early 1800s, travel by sea slowly changed too. Steamboats made traveling between continents much faster.

The explosion of the steamboat
Sultana in 1865

But traveling by sea was still risky. It was not uncommon for the parts that powered steamboats to explode from the buildup of too much pressure and heat. And large rocks and chunks of wood would often damage ships while they were at sea.

A combustion engine in 1872

These new ways to travel by land and sea sparked more ideas about how to travel to different parts of the world. They also helped bring about new tools to get there, like the **combustion** engine.

Combustion engines use fuel sources, like gasoline, to work. And they produce more power than steam engines. They power cars, and they were key to the Wright brothers getting an airplane to fly.

German inventor Karl Benz driving his first car with a combustion engine in 1886

Take to the Skies

Even with animals, bicycles, ships, cars, and trains available, there were still people who believed a better way to travel existed. What if humans could fly?

A few of the first serious attempts at flight actually took place in the late 1700s and involved hot air balloons made by the Montgolfier brothers. But the French duo found it difficult to control where a balloon went after it was in the air.

Many thought human travel by air was impossible—but not Orville and Wilbur Wright.

The two brothers liked to build and fix things. In fact, while growing up, Orville enjoyed taking items apart to see if he could learn how they worked.

By the time they were adults, Orville and Wilbur were interested in different kinds of **machines**. Orville started a **printing press** in 1886. Wilbur would later become his partner. In 1892, they opened a bicycle repair and sales shop.

Wilbur working in his bicycle shop in 1897

The knowledge the Wright brothers gained from running the bicycle shop helped them to better understand **aerodynamics**. They also used their earnings from the shop to pay for their next pursuit—flying.

First, the brothers experimented with **gliders**. But once gasoline engines became available, they determined they would need an engine that was strong enough to power a vehicle, but light enough that an aircraft would still be able to take flight. They would end up building their own engine.

The engine the Wright brothers
used in their 1903 airplane

In fewer than 10 years, the Wright brothers solved this problem using the skills they had gained making and repairing bicycles and gliders. In 1900, they asked the U.S. Weather Bureau about a place that was windier than where they lived in Dayton, Ohio. That place was Kitty Hawk, North Carolina.

Kitty Hawk, North Carolina

Wilbur flying in a glider
at Kitty Hawk in 1902

The next year, Orville and Wilbur started testing a series of flying inventions there. They would continue experimenting for almost three years.

On December 17, 1903, the Wright brothers changed history. Orville flew their airplane successfully. They were able to fly very short distances four times that day. The longest trip was when Wilbur flew their plane for 59 seconds.

But the plane was badly damaged by wind after that flight's landing, so nearly a year passed before the brothers were flying again.

In 1909, they started the Wright Company, which made airplanes for customers like the U.S. Army.

A military plane made by the Wright brothers

Other inventors quickly began to use the science and technology Orville and Wilbur had been successful with. By 1915, several airplane **manufacturers** existed. They began to build bigger, more complex airplanes than the Wright brothers' airplanes. So later that year, Orville sold the company.

A German airplane in 1915

A passenger airplane in
Paris, France, in 1929

The next phase of airplane design focused on increasing the number of passengers. Early models usually only had seating for the pilot and maybe one other person. As the design of planes changed, so did their primary use.

Flying Higher

Passenger airplanes quickly became popular. People also started creating airlines to help manage travelers' needs and to transport them safely. Now, more than 1,000 airlines exist worldwide.

In 1930, airplanes started hiring women as flight attendants. Before that, the copilot helped passengers.

By 1938, more than one million people were traveling by air in the United States each year.

A 1920 flight on what would become American Airlines

Did You Know?

Ellen Church, a nurse from Iowa, became the first woman flight attendant in 1930. She wanted to be a pilot, but airlines didn't hire women as pilots at the time.

Passengers on a jet plane in 1948

Another big change occurred in 1939. The first jet took flight. Jets have a special kind of engine. They can fly faster and for longer distances. Most **commercial** airlines use jet planes.

Jet travel played a big role in helping scientists understand how to power and control rockets, which means the Wright brothers' experiments with airplanes eventually helped make going to space a reality too. Now, about 70 countries have space programs.

Did You Know?

In 1961, the Soviet Union completed the first successful manned space flight.

From traveling across the country in just a few hours to sending a person to space, none of it would be possible without the big dreams of the Wright brothers.

Timeline

1783 Joseph and Étienne Montgolfier launch the first hot air balloon flight in France.

1892 Orville and Wilbur Wright open Wright Cycle Exchange, a bicycle sales and repair shop.

1900 The Wright brothers design their first powered flying machine.

1903 Orville Wright completes the first successful flight in an airplane.

1909 Wilbur Wright creates the first airport in the U.S.—College Park Airport in Maryland.

1914 The first flight offered by an airline in the United States travels from St. Petersburg, Florida, to Tampa, Florida.

1939 German physicist Hans von Ohain designs the first jet.

1958 President Dwight D. Eisenhower creates the National Aeronautics and Space Administration (NASA).

1961 The Soviet Union successfully completes the first space flight with an astronaut.

Glossary

aerodynamics (air-oh-dy-NAM-iks)—the ability of something to move easily and quickly through the air

combustion (kuhm-BUS-chuhn)—the process of catching fire and burning

commercial (kuh-MUHR-shuhl)—having to do with money

glider (GLYE-dur)—a lightweight aircraft that flies by floating and rising on air currents instead of by engine power

machine (muh-SHEEN)—a piece of equipment that is used to do a job

manufacturer (man-yuh-FAK-chur-ur)—a person or company that makes products

printing press (PRIN-ting PRES)—a large machine that prints words onto paper; the machine presses paper against a metal plate that has ink on it

vehicle (VEE-hih-kuhl)—a machine that carries people and goods

Read More

Peterson, Megan Cooley. *Amelia Earhart's Final Flight.* North Mankato, MN: Capstone, 2022.

Werner, Rachel. *Alexander Graham Bell Invents the Telephone.* North Mankato, MN: Capstone, 2025.

Whipple, Annette. *The Story of the Wright Brothers: A Biography Book for New Readers.* Emeryville, CA: Rockridge Press, 2020.

Internet Sites

History Channel: Wright Brothers
history.com/topics/inventions/wright-brothers

National Air and Space Museum: The Wright Brothers
airandspace.si.edu/explore/stories/wright-brothers

National Geographic Kids: Taking Flight with the Wright Brothers
kids.nationalgeographic.com/history/article/wright-brothers

Index

About the Author

Rachel Werner is the author of three children's books by Capstone, *Floods* (2022), *Moving and Grooving to Filmore's Beat* (2023), and *The Glam World Tour* (2025), as well as the nonfiction middle grade title *Glow & Grow: A Brown Girl's Positive Body Guide* (Free Spirit, 2025). She is on faculty for Hugo House in Seattle, Lighthouse Writers Workshop in Denver, and the Loft Literary Center in Minneapolis, where she leads curricula to educate writers and content producers in marketing their work.